Do Literary Books Sell Fewer Copies than Genre Books?

And other questions related to the "literary" genre in response to sundry articles and comments in circulation.

Lancelot Schaubert

Copyright © 2025 by Lancelot Schaubert

All rights reserved.

No portion of this work may be used in any way to train, encourage, or proliferate the use of artificial intelligence. The works remain the property of the authors, directly and subsidiarily.

Schaubert, Lancelot

Do Literary Books Sell Fewer Copies than Genre Books? / Lancelot Schaubert

ISBN: 978-1-949547-19-1

LITERARY CRITICISM / Modern / 21st Century

ART / Business Aspects

LANGUAGE ARTS & DISCIPLINES / Writing / Business Aspects

Printed in the United States of America and worldwide

Do Literary Books Sell Fewer Copies than Genre Books?

Wonderfully thoughtful pieces and comments recently published on Substack and elsewhere — as well as my own paltry reflections and commentary upon them — have led to this monster of an article.

If you're simply here for a quicky answer to the question *Do Literary Books Sell Fewer Copies than Genre Books?*, *the answer at first blush seems to be a messy "no."* But Betteridge's law of headlines could have told you that. The question is *why*. Because we can answer the question so many ways: taxonomically, mathematically, philosophically, etc.

When you look closer, the answer isn't what you expect. Even if you expect the "no" because you know Betteridge's law. This is a *far* more complicated question than it seems at first blush, perhaps even unanswerable by the time we get to the end of this journey, which I argue is absolutely worth taking because of every issue and idea it touches. If we were comparing American car sales to subscription French equestrian lessons, we could probably make a pretty quick dollar-to-dollar comparison. But the moment you start saying something like "sales of fast cars," well I have to ask, does this include Geo Metros?

Not at first blush, until you look under the hood and see the Geo Metro Turbo out classing a souped up Honda Civic on the racetrack.

So it gets messy.

That in mind, several questions connect to the titular, but they seem to me to be structured as follows.

1. Do literary books sell fewer copies than genre books?
2. What counts as "literary"?
3. What counts as "genre"?
4. Do standard on-the-literary-shelf books sell more on an *average units per title and per week basis*?
5. This is the only reasonable metric since book publishing is basically a lottery in which no one at any level of the business knows what they're doing or what will work. At best, it's compared to "venture capital," which, again, is generally gambling. Only some versions allow for handicapping as you might find in poker, but only some.
6. Per week allows for long term sales numbers, not merely first month sales, any week from which could give a "bestseller" status.
7. Average per book, per genre may be impossible to determine with the

downfall of Author Earnings (unless an anonymous publishing professional wants to post some hard numbers in the comments), but we may have some ideas...
8. Related to this, do literary works have a fandom?
9. Do genre books have a stratification for what makes a literature of high achievement?
10. What constitutes a ghetto in genre, in age, in other "sales" categories?
11. What is a fandom good for, anyways?
12. What is the nature of the author?
13. How does a fandom always-already participate in the person and work of the author?
14. How might one steward this nature of a fandom?
15. Are *literary* works — as the term is used in modernism and post-modernity (not, I'll remind you, even in *metamodernism or pre-modernism*) — the norm? Or are genre works the norm?
16. What literary works can be classified as genre?
17. What genre works can be classified as literary?
18. Why do people even care?
19. Should you?

There are, likely, other questions related to these, but this is generally my train of thought on these issues.

Pre-ramble:

(this context is more relevant than it appears)

BEFORE WE BEGIN, I want to note that I try my best to read broadly, deeply. I memorize when I can (shoutout to Henry Oliver for your recent memorized poem). Sometimes I reread, but the book really has to capture the daily weather of my mind. Other times I'll give a book *exactly* 20% and if it doesn't catch me, I throw it across the room. Or, in C.S. Lewis's case with *Don Quixote*, out the window after scrawling *Never again* on the back.

Preferably in white sharpie.

Of course, on a 400,000 word book, 20% equates to 80,000 words (yes, Sanderson, I'm looking at you... but also you, Dostoevsky). I do that because if you don't get to the major inciting incident by 20%, you don't know what you're doing. I don't know what you're doing. No one does. Having been on the receiving end of a non-zero number of DNFs (did not finish reviews), I get it. Both ways.

That said, I also write in my copies of the Britannica Great Books and Harvard Classics and try to memorize my own outlines and the outlines of my masters when I'm at my best, which is seldom, but I'll also binge read *Gone Girl* and *Sun Eater* in one sitting. Speaking of which, I just finished *Sun Eater* and moved immediately to the translation of *Les Miserables* after reading Heaney's Beowulf (which, I'll argue in another piece, *is* the best intro to Beowulf contra a widely circulated piece). I read it on Coney Island before a Cyclones game because it's what I grabbed. How's that for hot summer reading.

And yet...

It was Nicholas Sparks's *The Notebook* that told me it wasn't just okay to be a man who read in Southern Illinois that is, once more with vigor, a book desert 25,000 miles large and 1.3 million souls deep. *The Notebook*, a story about a carpenter who writes and reads poetry, got this fourth generation carpenter to read and write poetry in high school *on my own time* and, based on my publishing credits on that front (particularly since I'm being cited and recited at an English alliterative meter conference for the alliterative revival), I suppose *The Notebook* paid off in at least one small academic literary way. So while we're here, please be civil and don't take a hot steaming dump on romance novels either, folks.

Also tip your server: it might be your meet cute.

I read *The Road* and *Brothers Karamazov* back to back in the year my Dad died at 65 (COVID, post-pandemic), which helped me realize that *Daddy Issues are Overrated*. I hardly read anything that year other than legal and administrative and IRS forms. (For the record, if you ever want to tailpipe a metric shitton of Borg-level paperwork in your wake, die). Other than a couple of audiobooks (Bram Stoker, Tennyson, etc.) I only read five other things that year: *Gokushufudo: The Way of House Husband 1* by Kousuke Ono (which is divine for those who know even a teensy bit of Japanese or manga culture), *Little Women* by Alcott (first time, for Tara), *How to be Your Own Literary Agent* by Richard Curtis (who is retired now and with whom I've had the pleasure of dialoging over email — he's a kind and wise gentleman who knew Harlan Ellison personally, my main reason for writing), *A Knight of Seven Kingdoms* (to scratch my *Winds of Winter* itch), *The Rime of the Ancient Mariner* (was, again, dealing with death), and the Hugo-winning novella by Sanderson in *Arcanum Unbound*. My Korean friends and friends who had been expats to Korea approved of that one.

That's all in a year I read maybe 10-20% of my normal pace. I'm a slow reader in a good year compared to many, partly due to my insatiable hypergraphism, partly due to rereading and note taking and memorizing. But even that tiny sampling in the year dad died, in the year when I felt like reading absolutely *nothing*, should show you what I mean: I do not — I *refuse* — to practice favoritism in my reading habits. I also try to verbally and epistolarily encourage writers, agents, editors, you name it. The *only* thing I have zero time for is favoritism — bigotry — in any form. I have always had an aversion to mean girl / mean boy attitudes wherever I find them — the desperate overactive disgust drive that leads someone on a hopeless quest for some gnostic "inner circle" that absolutely doesn't exist.

So I don't have patience for that kind of exclusivity because it's delusional. But you can find it anywhere at any point in the business, at any point in a readership, at any level or sector of society. I try never to be exclusionary on that level, however much others try to exclude. I suppose that makes me exclusionary of the exclusive. That's fine.

That said, one of the most lovely and inclusive literary readings I ever went to in NYC was run by two rising stars in the New School MFA community at the time named Luke Wiget and Sam Farahmand. This was a decade ago. They called this series drDoctor and managed to invite a rather insane slate of readers to hoof it out to Bushwick at this...

Gee...

I mean the place *said* it was a library. They *claimed* library status.

The Mellow Pages. It had the weirdest, most obscure collection of literary paraphernalia I've ever seen outside of some niche reading rooms at the NYPL. I have no idea how this establishment stayed in business. Probably by the sheer willpower of drDoctor patrons alone.

drDoctor would host one poet, one fictioneer, one essayist every month. Luke and Sam would pull out a cooler full of extremely cheap canned beer. Beer cheep enough I can't remember the name and haven't seen it since and you're reading someone whose brother drinks "Steak Taters And Gravy." Luke always had one in hand and one in the front pocket of his pearlsnap like a sidearm, his "backup beer". And I remember the first time I went to one, I had a hardback of a *very* popular fantasy novel I was reading. I was embarrassed for my first, last, and only time in my life because — due to some of the literary folk I'd met in the city earlier that week, including a couple who had read at drDoctor — I felt judged.

Luke asked me what I was doing. He immediately asked me to turn the cover out. He liked the book. He wasn't ashamed of it. They had genre readers now and again.

That same generosity of spirit was unilateral for him and for Sam. It was the only time I have ever been embarrassed of the genre and it took someone like Luke preaching my own message back. In my moment of weakness, I realized I'd been right all along.

It calls to mind the logic of a longer piece *On the Three Ways of Writing for Children*:

> 1. I reply with a *tu quoque*. Critics who treat *adult* as a term of approval, instead of as a merely descriptive term, cannot be adult themselves. To be concerned about being grown up, to admire the grown up because it is grown up, to blush at the suspicion of being childish; these things are the marks of childhood and adolescence. And in childhood and adolescence they are, in moderation, healthy symptoms. Young things ought to want to grow. But to carry on into middle life or even into early manhood this concern about being adult is a mark of really arrested development. **When I was ten, I read fairy tales in secret and would have been ashamed if I had been found doing so. Now that I am fifty I read them openly. When I be-**

came a man I put away childish things, including the fear of childishness and the desire to be very grown up.

2. The modern view seems to me to involve a false conception of growth. They accuse us of arrested development because we have not lost a taste we had in childhood. But surely arrested development consists not in refusing to lose old things but in failing to add new things? I now like hock, which I am sure I should not have liked as a child. But I still like lemon-squash. I call this growth or development because I have been enriched: where I formerly had only one pleasure, I now have two. But if I had to lose the taste for lemon-squash before I acquired the taste for hock, that would not be growth but simple change. **I now enjoy Tolstoy and Jane Austen and Trollope as well as fairy tales and I call that growth: if I had had to lose the fairy tales in order to acquire the novelists, I would not say that I had grown but only that I had changed**. A tree grows because it adds rings: a train doesn't grow by leaving one station behind and puffing on to the next. In reality, the case is stronger and more complicated than this. I think my growth is just as ap-

parent when I now read the fairy tales as when I read the novelists, for I now enjoy the fairy tales better than I did in childhood: being now able to put more in, of course I get more out. But I do not here stress that point. Even if it were merely a taste for grown-up literature added to an unchanged taste for children's literature, addition would still be entitled to the name 'growth', and the process of merely dropping one parcel when you pick up another would not. It is, of course, true that the process of growing does, incidentally and unfortunately, involve some more losses. But that is not the essence of growth, certainly not what makes growth admirable or desirable. If it were, if to drop parcels and to leave stations behind were the essence and virtue of growth, why should we stop at the adult? Why should not *senile* be equally a term of approval? Why are we not to be congratulated on losing our teeth and hair? Some critics seem to confuse growth with the cost of growth and also to wish to make that cost far higher than, in nature, it need be.

3. **The whole association of fairy tale and fantasy with childhood is local and accidental**. I hope everyone has read Tolkien's essay on Fairy Tales, which is

perhaps the most important contribution to the subject that anyone has yet made. *If* so, you will know already that, in most places and times, the fairy tale has not been specially made for, nor exclusively enjoyed by, children. It has gravitated to the nursery when it became unfashionable in literary circles, just as unfashionable furniture gravitated to the nursery in Victorian houses. In fact, many children do not like this kind of book, just as many children do not like horsehair sofas: and many adults do like it, just as many adults like rocking chairs. And those who do like it, whether young or old, probably like it for the same reason. And none of us can say with any certainty what that reason is. The two theories which are most often in my mind are those of Tolkien and of Jung.

According to Tolkien the appeal of the fairy story lies in the fact that man there most fully exercises his function as a 'subcreator'; not, as they love to say now, making a 'comment upon life' but making, so far as possible, a subordinate world of his own. Since, in Tolkien's view, this is one of man's proper functions, delight naturally arises whenever it is successfully performed. For Jung, fairy tale liberates Archetypes which dwell in the collective unconscious, and when we read a good fairy tale we are obeying the old precept 'Know thyself'. I would venture to add to this my own theory, not indeed of the kind as a whole, but of one feature in it: I mean, the presence of beings other than human which yet behave, in varying degrees, humanly: the giants and dwarfs and talking beasts. I believe these to be at least (for they may have many other sources of power and beauty) an admirable hieroglyphic which conveys psychology, types of character, more briefly than novelistic presentation and to readers whom novelistic presentation could not yet reach. Consider Mr Badger in *The Wind in the Willows* — *that* extraordinary amalgam of high rank, coarse manners, gruffness, shyness, and goodness. The child who has once met Mr Badger has ever afterwards, in its bones, a knowledge of humanity and of English social history which it could not get in any other way.

Of course as all children's literature is not fantastic, so all fantastic books need not be children's books. It is still possible, even in an age so ferociously anti-romantic as our own, to write fantastic stories for adults: **though you will usually need to have made a name in some more fashionable kind of literature before anyone**

will publish them. But there may be an author who at a particular moment finds not only fantasy but fantasy-for-children the exactly right form for what he wants to say.

The distinction is a fine one. His fantasies for children and his fantasies for adults will have very much more in common with one another than either has with the ordinary novel or with what is sometimes called 'the novel of child life'. Indeed the same readers will probably read both his fantastic 'juveniles' and his fantastic stories for adults. **For I need not remind such an audience as this that the neat sorting-out of books into age-groups, so dear to publishers, has only a very sketchy relation with the habits of any real readers. Those of us who are blamed when old for reading childish books were blamed when children for reading books too old for us. No reader worth his salt trots along in obedience to a time-table**.

The distinction, then, is a fine one: and I am not quite sure what made me, in a particular year of my life, feel that not only a fairy tale, but a fairy tale addressed to children, was exactly what I must write-or burst. Partly, I think, that this form permits, or compels you to leave out things I wanted to leave out. It compels you to throw all the force of the book into what was done and said. It checks what a kind, but discerning critic called 'the expository demon' in me. It also imposes certain very fruitful necessities about length.

I expanded on all of this in my piece ***Contra Graham :: the War to Define YA Meaning and Maturity,*** in response to a cynical piece on slate. But I want to draw attention to a few things, mindful of my emphasis:

1. There's the obvious critique that someone invested in "literature" cannot be grown up or a serious critic or an adult if they're invested in "young adult" or "fantasy" literature. This is, of course, childish reasoning: wanting to be a grown-up. It is to our shame that many *formally defined* genre books and young adult are not seriously considered for Pulitzers and Booker Prizes, for worthy novels have always existed in those categories. Consider that the Pulitzer Prize Winner *To Kill a Mockingbird,* when it was bought by J. B. Lippincott & Co. at the behest of Truman Capote, wasn't marketed as YA. And yet it's arguably the

bestsellingerestly young adult novel of all time — more than *The Hunger Games* and *The Cat in the Hat* **combined**.

2. Lewis says no reader worth his salt trots along in obedience to a time-table. As I say frequently and often later, that is still the case: the *readers* don't make these decisions. Marketers and *some* MFA programs and *many* award boards do.

3. **C.S. Lewis hilariously says you can't make a living writing fantasy or science fiction**. If there's anything to follow the argument about the cultural decline of the "literary" novel, it's this quote right here: ***that C.S. Lewis***thought speculative fiction in his time to be a less viable career path in literature, economically speaking. *Dear Mr. Narnia, I seriously doubt this was actually the case, for many reasons.* Look: I'm sure the Cambridge professor was still getting shamed by his peers for writing the stuff, but that's different than checking the frigging sales numbers. In fact, Lewis himself was jilted in a similar though not identical way to Hemingway. Or perhaps he didn't try that often. Only a few times did *The Magazine of Science Fiction and Fantasy* publish pieces from his

space trilogy and short stories, but it was in an era where folks made *bank* off the stuff:

In fact, in the February 1956 issues of SF&F, THESE were the writers with whom Lewis published *Shoddy Lands*alongside:

Blish, Knight, Beaumont, Pohl, AND Asimov. It's like a who's who of bestsellers and golden era writers. If you want the full scan of that entire 1956 issue, it's a wonderful time capsule and it's here.

So… it's possible Lewis was speaking out of his shame, even then, and hadn't entirely internalized and practiced his own arguments in a similar way to what he *believed* to be true about physical affection among men verses what he *acted* upon. (Of course, I wrote about that nonsexual possibility contra toxic masculinity in *Boys Kissing Boys,* so no need to rehearse the holy kiss argument here).

In any case, Lewis and the Magazine of Science Fiction and Fantasy in mind, I too was acting out of my shame at the drDoctor series that night rather than my true beliefs about this porous osmosis interpenetrating both the ideas of "literary" and "genre."

Luke Wiget moved away and works (last I checked) for the Country Music Hall of Fame in Nashville. drDoctor evolved.

Meanwhile, here in NYC, we still have inclusive folk at all levels and sectors and genres of the business and readership. You also have the exclusive kind who play favorites.

All of that dynamic — and personal history on my reading tastes — should explain some of my tone here and elsewhere, knowing what you now know about how much I loathe favoritism in any form wherever I find it.

1. Do literary books sell fewer copies than genre books?

This has grown rather difficult to assess since Author Earnings sold out to move to an exclusive Bloomberg terminal model. But in the two or so years prior to the pandemic, authors across the board had *excellent* data on literary and genre and nonfiction sales alike. There may be an argument that the Simon and Schuster case that exposed the inequities is a direct descendent from Author Earnings, though I don't have the forensic patience to wage that argument at the moment.

What I do have passion for at present is teasing out the nature of "literary sales" in order to wonder whether or not they really sell fewer copies than genre books in terms of average units per title within a given genre.

A. But what counts as literary?

There was a wonderful note by Neo Passćism in June about whether literary novels are genre fiction:

> There is no sense in which anyone can non-meretriciously claim that MFAs aren't their own form of genre fiction. And in practice, everyone who dishonestly protests this ends up confirming it in their next utterance, as soon as they bring up narrators "disappearing into" characters, any variant of "free indirect style," any intimation that psychological conflicts should be "intuited" through character action and dialogue rather than aggressively and directly stated by the narrator, etc. These are all clear GENRE FICTION constraints, in the same sense that setting something in a "secondary fantasy world" or insisting on the heroine getting together with the Byronic hero in the last scene of the last chapter, are genre fiction constraints.
>
> Raymond Carver is genre fiction.
> Barry Hannah is genre fiction.
> Marilynne Robinson is genre fiction.
> Lan Samantha Chang is genre fiction.
> If you are incapable of understanding this, there is no possibility of you producing anything worth reading.

To which I responded thusly, which will become relevant in a moment:

> As Terry Pratchett said, it's a special province of phantasie — **φαντασία** — the rendering visible of certain speculative philosophies.

That in mind, Michael Chabon's name was invoked in this entire process as some kind of an exemplar *literary* novelist selling worse than *genre* novelists.

Up front, let's disabuse ourselves of this nonsense:

I find this doubly interesting because of the nature of Chabon's career. Yes, in Kavalier and Clay they invent the character named *the Escapist* as a comic book character. One that was turned into a literal comic book.

But to what end?

To the end of the very nature of escape! To escape *Nazi Germany,* for crying out loud. Once more, with vigor, to understand the meaning of Chabon's *Escapist* we need to cite the entire Tolkien quote here because it seems that very, very few of those with the loudest voices on escapism here on Substack and in similar spaces have actually read *On Fairy Stories,* let alone digested its arguments prior to offering any reasonable counterpoint. I would be shocked if Chabon did not have exactly this passage in mind. He's here — he could tell us rather quickly:

> I will now conclude by considering Escape and Consolation, which are naturally closely connected. Though fairy-stories are of course by no means the only medium of Escape, they are today one of the most obvious and (to some) outrageous forms of "escapist" literature; and it is thus reasonable to attach to a consideration of them some considerations of this term "escape" in criticism generally.

I have claimed that Escape is one of the main functions of fairy-stories, and since I do not disapprove of them, it is plain that I do not accept the tone of scorn or pity with which "Escape" is now so often used: a tone for which the uses of the word outside literary criticism give no warrant at all. In what the misusers are fond of calling Real Life, Escape is evidently as a rule very practical, and may even be heroic. In real life it is difficult to blame it, unless it fails; in criticism it would seem to be the worse the better it succeeds.

Evidently we are faced by a misuse of words, and also by a confusion of thought. Why should a man be scorned if, finding himself in prison, he tries to get out and go home? Or if, when he cannot do so, he thinks and talks about other topics than jailers and prison-walls?

The world outside has not become less real because the prisoner cannot see it. In using escape in this way the critics have chosen the wrong word, and, what is more, they are confusing, not always by sincere error, the Escape of the Prisoner with the Flight of the Deserter. **Just so a Party-spokesman might have labelled departure from the misery of the Führer's or any other Reich and even criticism of it as treachery**. In the same way these critics, to make confusion worse, and so to bring into contempt their opponents, stick their label of scorn not only on to Desertion, but on to real Escape, and what are often its companions, Disgust, Anger, Condemnation, and Revolt. Not only do they confound the escape of the prisoner with the flight of the deserter; but they would seem to prefer the acquiescence of the "quisling" to the resistance of the patriot. To such thinking you have only to say "the land you loved is doomed" to excuse any treachery, indeed to glorify it.

For a trifling instance: not to mention (indeed not to parade) electric street-lamps of mass-produced pattern in your tale is Escape (in that sense). But it may, almost certainly does, proceed from a considered disgust for so typical a product of the Robot Age, that combines elaboration and ingenuity of means with ugliness, and (often) with inferiority of result. These lamps may be excluded from the tale simply because they are bad lamps; and it is possible that one of the lessons to be learnt from the story is the realization of this fact.**1**

But out comes the big stick: "Electric lamps have come to stay," they say. Long ago Chesterton truly remarked that, as soon as he heard that anything "had come to stay," he knew that it would be very soon replaced—indeed regarded as pitiably obsolete and shabby. "The march of Science, its tempo quickened by the needs of war, goes inexorably on ... making some things obsolete, and foreshadowing new developments in the utilization of electricity": an advertisement. This says the same thing only more menacingly. The electric street-lamp may indeed be ignored, simply because it is so insignificant and transient.

Fairy-stories, at any rate, have many more permanent and fundamental things to talk about. Lightning, for example. The escapist is not so subservient to the whims of evanescent fashion as these opponents. He does not make things (which it may be quite rational to regard as bad) his masters or his gods by worshipping them as inevitable, even "inexorable." And his opponents, so easily contemptuous, have no guarantee that he will stop there: he might rouse men to pull down the streetlamps. Escapism has another and even wickeder face: Reaction.

Not long ago—incredible though it may seem—I heard a clerk of Oxenford declare that he "welcomed" the proximity of mass-production robot factories, and the roar of self-obstructive mechanical traffic, because it brought his university into "contact with real life." He may have meant that the way men were living and working in the twentieth century was increasing in barbarity at an alarming rate, and that the loud demonstration of this in the streets of Oxford might serve as a warning that it is not possible to preserve for long an oasis of sanity in a desert of unreason by mere fences, without actual offensive action (practical and intellectual). I fear he did not.

In any case the expression "real life" in this context seems to fall short of academic standards. The notion that motor-cars are more "alive" than, say, centaurs or dragons is curious; that they are more "real" than, say, horses is pathetically absurd. How real, how startlingly alive is a factory chimney compared with an elm-tree: poor obsolete thing, insubstantial dream of an escapist!

For my part, I cannot convince myself that the roof of Bletchley station is more "real" than the clouds. And as an artefact I find it less inspiring than the legendary dome of heaven. The bridge to platform 4 is to me less interesting than Bifröst guarded by Heimdall with the Gjallarhorn. From the wildness of my heart I cannot exclude the question whether railway-engineers, if they had been brought up on more fantasy, might not have done better with all their abundant means than they commonly do.2 Fairy-stories might be, I guess, better Masters of Arts than the academic person I have referred to.

Much that he (I must suppose) and others (certainly) would call "serious" literature is no more than play under a glass roof by the side of a municipal swimming-bath.3 Fairy-stories may invent monsters that fly the air or dwell in the deep, but at least they do not try to escape from heaven or the sea.

And if we leave aside for a moment "fantasy," I do not think that the reader or the maker of fairy-stories need even be ashamed of the "escape" of archaism: of preferring not dragons but horses, castles, sailing-ships, bows and arrows;

not only elves, but knights and kings and priests.

For it is after all possible for a rational man, after reflection (quite unconnected with fairy-story or romance), to arrive at the condemnation, implicit at least in the mere silence of "escapist" literature, of progressive things like factories, or the machine-guns and bombs that appear to be their most natural and inevitable, dare we say "inexorable," products.

"The rawness and ugliness of modern European life"—that real life whose contact we should welcome —"is the sign of a biological inferiority, of an insufficient or false reaction to environment." The maddest castle that ever came out of a giant's bag in a wild Gaelic story is not only much less ugly than a robot-factory, it is also (to use a very modern phrase) "in a very real sense" a great deal more real. Why should we not escape from or condemn the "grim Assyrian" absurdity of top-hats, or the Morlockian horror of factories? They are condemned even by the writers of that most escapist form of all literature, stories of Science fiction. These prophets often foretell (and many seem to yearn for) a world like one big glass-roofed railway-station. But from them it is as a rule very hard to gather what men in such a world-town will do.

They may abandon the "full Victorian panoply" for loose garments (with zip-fasteners), but will use this freedom mainly, it would appear, in order to play with mechanical toys in the soon-cloying game of moving at high speed. To judge by some of these tales they will still be as lustful, vengeful, and greedy as ever; and the ideals of their idealists hardly reach farther than the splendid notion of building more towns of the same sort on other planets. It is indeed an age of "improved means to deteriorated ends."

It is part of the essential malady of such days—producing the desire to escape, not indeed from life, but from our present time and self-made misery—that we are acutely conscious both of the ugliness of our works, and of their evil. So that to us evil and ugliness seem indissolubly allied. We find it difficult to conceive of evil and beauty together. The fear of the beautiful fay that ran through the elder ages almost eludes our grasp. Even more alarming: goodness is itself bereft of its proper beauty. In Faerie one can indeed conceive of an ogre who possesses a castle hideous as a nightmare (for the evil of the ogre wills it so), but one cannot conceive of a house built with a good purpose—an inn, a hostel for travellers, the hall of a virtuous and noble king—that is yet sickeningly ugly. At the present day it would be rash to hope to see one that was not—unless it was built before our time.

This, however, is the modern and special (or accidental) "escapist" aspect of fairy-stories, which they share with romances, and other stories out of or about the past. Many stories out of the past have only become "escapist" in their appeal through surviving from a time when men were as a rule delighted with the work of their hands into our time, when many men feel disgust with man-made things.

But there are also other and more profound "escapisms" that have always appeared in fairy-tale and legend. There are other things more grim and terrible to fly from than the noise, stench, ruthlessness, and extravagance of the internal-combustion engine. There are hunger, thirst, poverty, pain, sorrow, injustice, death.4 And even when men are not facing hard things such as these, there are ancient limitations from which fairy-stories offer a sort of escape, and old ambitions and desires (touching the very roots of fantasy) to which they offer a kind of satisfaction and consolation. Some are pardonable weaknesses or curiosities: such as the desire to visit, free as a fish, the deep sea; or the longing for the noiseless, gracious, economical flight of a bird, that longing which the aeroplane cheats, except in rare moments, seen high and by wind and distance noiseless, turning in the sun: that is, precisely when imagined and not used.

There are profounder wishes: such as the desire to converse with other living things. On this desire, as ancient as the Fall, is largely founded the talking of beasts and creatures in fairy-tales, and especially the magical understanding of their proper speech. This is the root, and not the "confusion" attributed to the minds of men of the unrecorded past, an alleged "absence of the sense of separation of ourselves from beasts." A vivid sense of that separation is very ancient; but also a sense that it was a severance: a strange fate and a guilt lies on us. Other creatures are like other realms with which Man has broken off relations, and sees now only from the outside at a distance, being at war with them, or on the terms of an uneasy armistice. There are a few men who are privileged to travel abroad a little; others must be content with travellers' tales. Even about frogs. In speaking of that rather odd but widespread fairy-story The Frog-King Max Müller asked in his prim way: "How came such a story ever to be invented? Human beings were, we may hope, at all times sufficiently enlightened to know that a marriage between a frog and the daughter of a queen was absurd." Indeed we may hope so! For if not, there would be no point in this story at all, depending as it does essentially on the sense of the absurdity.

Folk-lore origins (or guesses about them) are here quite beside the point. It is of little avail to consider totemism. For certainly, whatever customs or beliefs about frogs and wells lie behind this story, the frog-shape was and is preserved in the fairy-story precisely because it was so queer and the marriage absurd, indeed abominable. Though, of course, in the versions which concern us, Gaelic, German, English, there is in fact no wedding between a princess and a frog: the frog was an enchanted prince. **And the point of the story lies not in thinking frogs possible mates, but in the necessity of keeping promises (even those with intolerable consequences) that, together with observing prohibitions, runs through all Fairyland. This is one of the notes of the horns of Elfland, and not a dim note.**

And lastly there is the oldest and deepest desire, the Great Escape: the Escape from Death.

Fairy-stories provide many examples and modes of this—which might be called the genuine escapist, or (I would say) fugitive spirit. But so do other stories (notably those of scientific inspiration), and so do other studies. Fairy-stories are made by men not by fairies. The Human-stories of the elves are doubtless full of the Escape from Deathlessness. But our stories cannot be expected always to rise above our common level. They often do. Few lessons are taught more clearly in them than the burden of that kind of immortality, or rather endless serial living, to which the "fugitive" would fly. For the fairy-story is specially apt to teach such things, of old and still today. Death is the theme that most inspired George MacDonald.5

Again, all of this as the context of Chabon writing about *The Escapist*. And he's proffered as some qualitative contrast with *genre* fiction?!

In addition, you're talking about the man who wrote the story for *Spider Man 2* and *John Carter*. He worked on *Star Trek*. He pitched stories for *X-men* and *Fantastic Four*. And to top it all off, *The Yiddish Policeman's Union* is an alt history of the relocation set in Sitka, Alaska. *The Yiddish Policemen's Union* won a number of science fiction awards: the Nebula Award for Best Novel, the Locus Award for Best SF Novel, the Hugo Award for Best Novel, and the Sidewise Award for Alternate History for Best Novel. It was shortlisted for the British Science Fiction Association Award for Best Novel and the Edgar Allan Poe Award for Best Novel. And, published only seven years later, it has sold less than half the units of *Kavalier,* which is about the pace you would expect for a novel with seven fewer years of sales under its belt.

So what — on earth — do we even mean with these meaningless genre distinctions for an author who can so quickly pass from literary to scifi and fantasy? Who defended escapism with the same arguments that Tolkien wielded *inside the text* of his Pulitzer Prize winning novel? Who wrote for the fandom's films? Who won all the spec fic awards?

Similarly, consider Emily St. John Mandell's project, *Station Eleven,* which was originally recommended to me by the critic Porter Anderson in person at a retreat in Salem, Massachusetts. I adored that book, for reasons I explained in *Hopeful Apocalypses,* but also because fundamentally St. John Mandell wrote an apologetic for science fiction in the way that Chabon wrote one for fantasy. Not only does she show how deeply science fiction helps us envision a way out of our current predicament; how it is the start of the scientific method; how it does, in fact, begin the entire process of speculative philosophy, which I argued for in *A Brief History of Science Fiction from Antiquity to 2024* — she also shows how the fundamental mythos of the New World ideology **is** science fiction. That is to say if you — reading this — have anything at all you like about the Americas as an ideal nation state, northern hemisphere or southern, you are a direct *real world* descendent of *speculative fiction.*

You are living *in the literal escapism, right now*.

B. What counts as genre?

This is where it gets even more ridiculous. Better than *Girl Interrupted, Go Ask Alice,* and *I Never Promised You a Rose Garden* is Patrick Rothfuss's *The Slow Regard of Silent Things*. But many "literary" folk still haven't encountered it because it sits on the "fantasy" shelf.

It has no plot.

To emphasize how thoroughly it has no plot, I would like to highlight the top rated one-star review of this book on Goodreads:

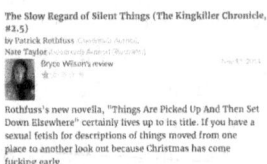

AND THIS ONE is like it:

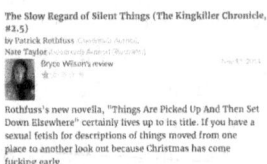

It's ENTIRELY about a girl's interior world living in the Underthing beneath a major university and her best friends are all inanimate objects like bottle caps. It's wild and remains my favorite piece by him, partly because — among other things — the title is the dictionary definition of the verb "to moon," which only makes sense to deep and long readers of the book. Though, to students of the history of the word lunacy, the title might make sense.

It's wonderful. And it's generally ignored by the precise crowd who would adore it the most.

Moving the other way, as I said on a comment in *Highbrow literature has acquired a fandom. To succeed, writers need to manage it* by the ever insightful and present Naomi Kanakia, it's almost as if genre readers have been intelligent all along and there's no such thing as "literary" fiction except a desperate clinging to some imagined caste. It's almost as if "literary" readers — the actual buyers of books — read both and only blush when someone tries to publicly shame them for reading "garbage." Literary writers actively write genre, genre writers often float into a higher register of prose. I already mentioned Rothfuss, but so many others have been later "accepted" as literary, whatever that means, once time had done its work. Could not the same be said of literary stories accepted as genre? Especially mindful of Neo-Passéism's and Tolkien's discussion above?

Midsummer Night's Dream and *Moby Dick* are fantasy and they're read by "literary" and "low brow" readers alike, I meet these readers at spec fic conventions and in MFA programs.

Jane Austin and Edith Wharton write romance, read by all sorts of readers.

The Road and *A Canticle for Leibowitz* are both apocalyptic science fiction novels, ready by all sorts. *The Road,* in particular, as I wrote elsewhere is simply Cormac McCarthy's retelling of Dante's *Inferno*, which the Eastern Orthodox philosopher David Bentley Hart very popularly called out as speculative *fiction* when compared to the long history of universalist readings of scripture, the Eastern fathers, and other theologians in his controversial work *That All Shall Be Saved.* Personally, I don't find it that controversial to call Dante's Divine Comedy a midlife crisis self-insert Virgil torture fanfic, namely because that's literally how Dante begins the book. It's a book about Dante's journey, no one else's, and whatever it is, it's fiction and it's speculative philosophy. Do the math on that one.

People forget, as I said in my piece on *Travels with Charlie,* that Steinbeck's first novel was a pirate fantasy and his second novel was a werewolf thriller. They forget that Hemingway felt jilted by the spec fic magazines: he wasn't good enough to sell to the pulps.

Think about that for a moment. Really take two seconds and think: is it harder to do everything a literary novel does? Or harder to do all of that *and then do it inside the confines of an invented secondary world with alternative physics, weather, and whatever else?*

Some want to be seen as academic, seen as smart, have honors and awards and the privilege that comes with prestige. Or the power connected to it. Or the pleasure of trading favors for being inside some sort of gnostic inner circle. I once saw a very famous novelist here in Brooklyn at a reading attended entirely by students who said — openly, loudly — that the best part of being a lauded literary novelist was the sexual favors she got. To underage students this old woman said this. I was mortified and raised my voice to the hosts.

But these are all proximate goods (or ills, in her case). They are not beauty, truth, and goodness. They're irrelevant to what great books are actually trying to *do* and *be*. They may or may not carry on the great conversation, focused as they are on those proximate ends.

These readers (i.e. all readers) are incredibly intelligent and they don't have *discriminating* tastes in the sense of genre. What they have is *discerning* taste: a much better sense for bullshit than the average critic for two simple reasons (1) they're not worried about their own careers in literature or media, generally, (2) they're curious and joyful with the things they like and don't mind telling you what's good and what sucked. It will be their grandchildren, not ours, who determine what becomes a classic. Things do fall in and out of favor, you see.

Remember: Dickens was a mere popular writer whom most people considered a hack until, of all people, Chesterton defended him critically. We now assign Dickens in school.

Oh and by the way, much of his stuff was speculative fiction. Or what else do you call *A Christmas Carol*? "Marley was dead to begin with" is immediately refuted in any naturalistic way with Scrooge's five-senses experience. It's a phenomenology of death and its meaning as well as life after death and, as N.T. Wright would say, life *after* "life after death."

In this way, plenty of genre writers believe it's their job to improve the reader. Plenty of literary writers attempt genre without having any knowledge of the field and truly believe, for instance, that they're the first one to invent a time traveling super soldier (only to invite the litigious wrath of the dessicated corpse of one Harlan Ellison) or a nonlinear narrative about a plague or *The Rules of Magic*, which had no magic system, no rules, and no real magic per se. If anything, there's an ignorance in the literary crowd of the foundational works of literature that isn't present in the genre crowd because, for whatever reason, American lit has been tidally locked around 20th century cynicism for the last century.

It's eating its own tail.

Don't believe me?

Take a look at all of the Pulitzer Prize winners for fiction. Ask yourself: in recent years, how many of these are remakes or riffs on classic works of literature as opposed to new stories? Certainly that's allowed — there's something downright medieval in a good way about trying to get your version of, for instance, Arthur or Virgil right — but almost all of them are remakes. *The Road* was Dante's Inferno as I said. *March* was Allcot. *Gilead* was the retelling of the Abraham / Sara story. *James* was Mark Twain. *Demon Copperhead* was Dickens.

This isn't a bad thing, but its direct parallel is Hollywood remakes.

We have stopped looking forwards. All of us, that is, but the genre writers and the readers who truly do not care about these distinctions without difference meant only to sell more books to a specific crowd. Readers are RAVENOUS for good, new stories. They have no bias about origin. No one's asking about artisanal culinary experience when they're starving. Ask yourself: when was the last time you read an award winning literary novel that looked *real* poverty in the eye? Our readers will always be hungry — this is why great screenplays always set the pace for blockbusters.

I now have the privilege of knowing a brilliant producer who lives in the Hamptons. She reads classics. She reads Game of Thrones. She reads Pulitzer Prize winners. She reads romance. She reads memoir. She doesn't care, she reads it all, and she's that kind of oldschool, blunt, smoker New York lady who will tell you exactly what she thinks and why: she has the literary pedigree to know it all and to deconstruct or exalt it equally. She does. She doesn't care. She's no respecter of awards or sales or whatever.

If the folks in this business stopped talking down to people like her (she — a very educated, wealthy, and powerful reader!), erased the completely arbitrary boundary line, and saw that *most* readers don't care for the genre distinction at all, they would actually revive both sides of the publishing industry. Both sides would benefit because there aren't sides from the reader's perspective. There are merely "books."

What's hilarious is that *most authors* are also these kinds of readers, as Chabon's work and St. John Mandell's work and Rothfuss's work shows. If we know anything about Stephen King, is that the man reads a lot and that he's no respecter of persons. He judged *The Best American Short Stories* in the exact same year he published a story about a miracle worker, another about a mute crime, and a third port-a-potty escape horror. He also, according to the editor, (1) read more stories than any other guest editor she'd had and (2) seemed to lobby for more *genre* stories than they'd ever had nominated. They published one (1). And only from the Magazine of Science Fiction & Fantasy.

It's hard, of course, to stop arguing about this distinction without difference because both political parties thrive on the arbitrary distinction between "coastal elite" and "rural ignorance." Both pride themselves on their side. And the genre/literary divide seems a bit of a kissing cousin with this bad idea. It's certainly just as inbred.

Because neither paints the truth of things. As Emerson said, "The city is recruited from the country." We are interdependent. We are interpenetrated with one another. We are, in a way, dually consubstantial and always-already elite while always-already ignorant; always-already urban while always-already rural. The city eats rural food. The rural folk come to the city for baseball games. It's Bourdain eating foie gras at some bougie restaurant and then Bourdain again later that night eating corn dogs on the back of a pickup with his film crew. It's De Blasio in the mayor's mansion and De Blasio again riding the broken down subway in Sunset Park. It's an endless cycle, voyage and return, and it cuts right through literature.

Literature merely means "written works" as in "letter" or "letter of the law."

Do Literary Books Sell Fewer Copies than Genre Book...

To be "literary" is anything related to the written word.

That includes all genres and includes all readers, most of whom read both"

Is there Now go back 150 years prior to 1962. What do you find?

Now another 150. What do you find?

Now another.

Now another.

Do that twenty times. Average it out by genre.

Still mostly Wouk and Salinger types? Or are they exemplars of 20th century outliers from the international, historical baseline?

I could go on and on about this, but I'm *always* reminded in these discussions of the interview The Onion did with Terry Pratchett back in 1995 that Patrick Rothfuss unearthed for us:

> "O: You're quite a writer. You've a gift for language, you're a deft hand at plotting, and your books seem to have an enormous amount of attention to detail put into them. You're so good you could write anything. Why write fantasy?
>
> "Pratchett: I had a decent lunch, and I'm feeling quite amiable. That's why you're still alive. I think you'd have to explain to me why you've asked that question.
>
> "O: It's a rather ghettoized genre.
>
> "P: This is true. I cannot speak for the US, where I merely sort of sell okay. But in the UK I think every book— I think I've done twenty in the series—

since the fourth book, every one has been one the top ten national bestsellers, either as hardcover or paperback, and quite often as both. Twelve or thirteen have been number one. I've done six juveniles, all of those have nevertheless crossed over to the adult bestseller list. On one occasion I had the adult best seller, the paperback best-seller in a different title, and a third book on the juvenile bestseller list. Now tell me again that this is a ghettoized genre.

"O: It's certainly regarded as less than serious fiction.

"P: (Sighs) Without a shadow of a doubt, the first fiction ever recounted was fantasy. Guys sitting around the campfire— Was it you who wrote the review? I thought I recognized it— Guys sitting around the campfire telling each other stories about the gods who made lightning, and stuff like that. They did not tell one another literary stories. They did not complain about difficulties of male menopause while being a junior lecturer on some midwestern college campus. Fantasy is without a shadow of a doubt the ur-literature, the spring from which all other literature has flown. Up to a few hundred years ago no one would have disagreed with this, because most stories were, in some sense, fantasy. Back in the middle ages, people wouldn't have thought twice about bringing in Death as a character who would have a role to play in the story. Echoes of this can be seen in Pilgrim's Progress, for example, which hark back to a much earlier type of storytelling. The epic of Gilgamesh is one of the earliest works of literature, and by the standard we would apply now— a big muscular guys with swords and certain godlike connections— That's fantasy. The national literature of Finland, the Kalevala. Beowulf in England. I cannot pronounce Bahaghvad-Gita but the Indian one, you know what I mean. The national literature, the one that underpins everything else, is by the standards that we apply now, a work of fantasy.

"Now I don't know what you'd consider the national literature of America, but if the words Moby Dick are inching their way towards this conversation, whatever else it was, it was also a work of fantasy. Fantasy is kind of a plasma in which other things can be carried. I don't think this is a ghetto. This is, fantasy is, almost a sea in which other genres swim. Now it may be that there has developed in the last couple of hundred years a subset of fantasy which merely uses a different icongraphy, and that is, if you like, the serious literature, the Booker Prize contender. Fantasy can be serious literature. Fantasy has often been serious literature. You have to fairly dense to think that Gulliver's Travels is only a story about a guy having a real fun time among big people and little people and horses and stuff like that. What the book was about was something else. Fantasy can carry quite a serious burden, and so can humor. So what you're saying is, strip away the trolls and the dwarves and things and put everyone into modern dress, get them to agonize a bit, mention Virginia Woolf a few times, and there! Hey! I've got a serious novel. But you don't actually have to do that.

"(Pauses) That was a bloody good answer, though I say it myself."

Do you want to be wise?
Would you like to be academic on this issue?
Would you like to be seen as someone who is literary, well read, or understanding?
Ignore the distinction without difference.
Ignore the classes and castes.
They're just people.
Writing fiction.
Drink deep.
Read wide.

C. Do standard on-the-literary shelf books sell more or less than genre books when it comes to an *average units per title and per week basis?*

This is easier to determine than the broader idea of average units per book per genre for two reasons (1) this requires the huge sample size of Author Earnings and, unless someone can give me access to that, I'll be operating in ignorance as well as (2) the very real genre pliability shown above first in §1a, then in §1b.

However, the average units per title and per week basis give us some very clear indicators.

On *The Cultural Decline of Literary Fiction* by Owen Yingling, Sherman Alexie commented the following:

> Approximately ten years ago, I was in the office of a well-known editor who'd published one of the most talked-about, well-reviewed, and award-winning literary novels of that year. And I was shocked to learn that it has sold less than 10,000 copies. I cussed in disbelief. And the editor said. "Sherman, those are good numbers."

Evan Marc Katz responded:

> I remember reading this about Kavalier and Klay (*sic*); it won all the awards and sold, like, 30,000 copies.

At this point I had to chime in, not least because — as I said above — Kavalier and *Clay* not only argues for the positives and realities of escapism, nor because it was written by a man who clearly has a passion, a skill, and a knowledge of the history of genre works and who has won all of the awards for genre contributions and who has invested in the community through frigging Star Trek and Spiderman and his own damn comic based on said Pulitzer Prize winning novel's positively Escapist hero.

More importantly, I *also* had to chime in because the comparison was flat wrong on a basic *math* level:

> Actually, based on the Goodreads data, Kavalier and Clay has now sold about 800,000 copies. Sometimes it's simply a long-tail thing.

Evan responded:

> Yeah, but I think at the time he won, sales were still comparatively anemic compared to actual bestsellers.

So I said:

> Sure, that may very well be. But… I… really don't think that's contextually any different than genre sales, given the context of comparing literary books to genre books. Kavalier and Clay averages out to 667 per week as a backlist book over two

and a half decades is actually something I'd personally prefer to 5,000-10,000 in a given week.

Moreover, Jim Butcher — who but for his first book — posts a nearly identical number of units for the books of the Dresden Files and makes bestseller lists consistently. That includes vol. 2 which came out within the same time frame as Kavalier and Clay and sold an almost identical number of units in that 25-year span. Butcher did not have these equivalent sales numbers until later books came out (which K&C had), later books won Hugo nominations, Dragon awards, television adaptations, etc.

And Butcher's one of the bestseller exemplars for urban fantasy — his agency DMLA makes *sure* folks know that. So if we're not comparing apples to apples, then what exactly are we doing here?

This is what I mean.

We're not playing fair with the semiotic square of meaning here. It's sort of like when someone from the Occident says "all Muslims are terrorists" or from the Middle East says "all Christians are KKK lynchers" or crusaders who sack Constantinople in 1204 (Istanbul, if you want to be pedantic) for that matter — it's not being fair with the totality of the category nor the specificity of said terrorists, said lynchers, said crusaders (who in the Constantinople case, were Latin mercenaries murdering Greek Orthodox), or said jihadists (who in some cases were even under the employment of, say, Michael VIII Palaiologos right alongside kilt-wearing axe-wielding Celts during his attempt to retake Constantinople).

It's not comparing like to like, let alone assuming the best of a given category, nor nuance, etc.

Assuming, of course, that these categories *are* or *ever should be* in competition — and pretending for a moment through a herculean act of escapism as if all books are not some panoply of genre combinations that, once the total account of their accidents are settled and balanced, end as a monotypic taxon that contains the species of exactly **one** book, a direct literary analog to homo sapiens themselves; books being as Milton said the "precious life-blood of a master spirit, embalmed and treasured up on purpose to a life beyond life" — we ought to compare the long tail sales of the best literary works with the long tail sales of the best genre works, released in the same year. Butcher's work and Chabon's work *in the same year* is a great example, assuming we set aside all of the *significant* reservations I have about excluding Chabon from the genre category or Rothfuss from the literary category.

We need to also compare the worst selling with the worst selling. I think — other than indy Kindle romance, which is the massive sleeping-with-you giant almost no one ever mentions who doesn't write it or work for Harlequin — we may find them comparable.

In the case of the worst, *most books — categorically* — sell a thousand copies. Many sell none or a dozen in their lifetime, particularly indies in Ama-

Do Literary Books Sell Fewer Copies than Genre Book...

zon's long tail. But gobs of them counted in the "dozen" category *in a given year* from the Simon and Schuster case have over a million *lifetime* sales.6 So it's tricky. Sure, Chabon's book sold only a handful that year. But he's easily up to close to a million sales by now. Same thing goes with the genres. How do you count a backlist you can't see?

Which is to say, how do you catalog and audit the entire history of every book published, adored, reread, treasured, archived, ruined, burned?

The only thing we can say for sure, best books and worst books alike, is that far more books are published in the genre categories than otherwise. But then when we start considering how many literary novels compete as genre novels (like *Yiddish Policeman*) and how many genre novels rise to the level of highbrow literature (like *Slow Regard, Midsummer Night's Dream*), the only thing we can determine is that these labels are simply used to find a novel's public. How do you find a novel's public? Well for those keeping score, about 10,000 copies is the best shot at making that happen that because:

1. If 10,000 people read it, there's a 50% chance 25,000 will
2. If 25,000 people read it, there's a 50% chance 50,000 will
3. If 50,000 people read it, there's a 50% chance 100,000 will
4. If 100,000 people read it, there's a 50% chance 250,000 will
5. If 250,000 people read it, there's a 50% chance 500,000 will

6. If 500,000 people read it, there's a 50% chance 1mil will
7. —

So it goes.

THE KEY IS FINDING 10,000 people to read it, even if you have to give it away to that first 10k. Other than that, yeah — fickleness plus stubbornness plus time in hopes that word of mouth in the right places gets it to click. More books, more attempts, more chances.

Why not use genre or lackthereof to help find said public?

Short of that, what do we really mean with any of these labels?

Yet, I'll try. Frustrated as I am with the impossibility of the project, I'll take a swing at the wild pitch because I'm that crazy kind of scrappy, fast, base stealing bunter:

i. This *"average units per title and per week basis"* is the only reasonable metric since book publishing is basically a lottery in which no one at any level of the business knows what they're doing or what will work.

At best, it's compared to "venture capital," which, again, is glorified gambling. Only some versions allow for handicapping as you might find in poker, but only some.

It's fine if you don't believe me.

Read these tweets by Alec Shane, the literary agent from Writer's House who was mentored by Stephenie Meyer's agent:

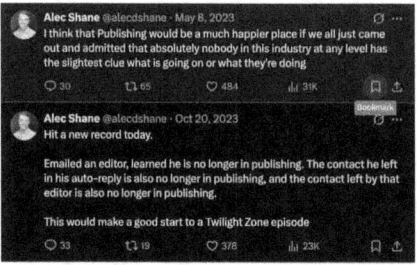

His disposition was confirmed by the S&S court case.

ii. *Per week units* allows for long term sales numbers, not merely first month sales or any week from which could have given a "bestseller" status.

This can be taken by the standard formula of 4x Goodreads ratings (which is *eerily* accurate, most of the time) and divided by the number of weeks out. I will make some significant disclaimers and observations before I show you the list:

- There is *very* likely a kind of recency bias to logging books on Goodreads. Certainly the Aristotle revival in Medieval Europe will not be properly logged in book sales. However, we should expect that to track with a sort of logarithmic curve towards the present, away from the past, so that it correlates. This is why I included the dates of the books: generally speaking, but for outliers, most books published in the past are simply being read less than most books published in the present. Or reprinted (as in the case with *To Kill a Mockingbird* or *A Wrinkle in Time*).
- The average per week should show these parallels, so this is why I did them in couplets: two books from the sixties, two from the eighties, two from the fifties, four from the eighties, two from the early twentieth century. Again, it's an average per week from date of publication. So with Mary Poppins,

we're talking 138,807 ratings x 4 to get 555228 and then ÷ by 4775 weeks since it was first published January 1, 1934.

- That in mind, it's pretty much identical, perhaps in a given year one genre will be favored over another, but it's wildly inconsistent the further you go and it certainly doesn't look anything like a trend in my estimation — it's almost as random as the books themselves, which tells us again that a story rises and falls on its own merit as well as some stochastic effects of word-of-mouth and similar opportunity factors indiscriminate of genre. Book sales rise and fall, people like what they like, they're selling across categories. And, as I said, the genres blur. *The Road* is a post apocalyptic novel. *Lonesome Dove* is a cowboy novel. Wharton wrote romance. Etc.
- This also means that in whatever lane you pick, there are breakout novels, backlist novels that get popular over time, midlist novels, and duds in terms of sales. No award, no genre fandom, no film deal will compensate for one that just won't outsell another. And yet you find almost identical trends among both in identical time spans in a way.

From here we get something like this, when

comparing the Pulitzer Prize winners to the most popular genre books released within a year or two:

Compare Pulitzers to Genre:

1. *To Kill a Mockingbird* — 7867 per week (1960)
2. *A Wrinkle in Time* — 1522 per week (1962)

1. *The Road* — 4074 per week (2006)
2. *Old Man's War* — 905 per week (2007)

1. *The Old Man and the Sea* — 1315 per week (1952)
2. *Fahrenheit 451* — 2893 per week (1953)

1. *A Confederacy of Dunces* — 494 per week (1980)
2. *The Restaurant at the End of the Universe* — 529 per week (1980)

1. *Lonesome Dove* — 417 per week (1985)
2. *Speaker for the Dead* — 519 per week (1986)

1. *The Age of Innocence* — 138 *per week* (1920)
2. *Mary Poppins* — 116 *per week* (1934)

1. *The Killer Angels* — 134 *per week* (1974)
2. *The Sword of Shanarra* — 158 *per week* (1977)* ← **this includes a double recency bias: 3 less years of sales AND a recent TV series adaptation and it's still about the same as Killer Angels**

1. *The Stone Diaries* — 97 *per week* (1995)
2. *Interesting Times* — 142 *per week* (1994) ← **this Pratchett disparity might be the greatest of the set**

COMPARE **Booker Prize Winners to Genre:**

1. *Life of Pi* — 5549 *per week* (9/11/2001) ← *aside from the fascinating release date, which could be its own post, it's also pretty clearly about*

speculative fiction, though making the opposite argument as Chabon
2. *American Gods* — 3117 per week (2001)

1. *The God of Small Things* — 858 per week (1997)
2. *The Green Mile* — 910 per week (1996)

1. *The Bone People* — 43 per week (1984)
2. *Moreta: Dragonlady of Pern* — 55 per week (1984)

1. *Midnight's Children* — 225 per week (1981)
2. *The Mist* — 297 per week (1980)

1. *Oscar and Lucinda* — 44 per week (1988)
2. *The Fifth Child* — 47 per week (1988) <– note that I was born in 1987, the year of the crash, and both of these here may reflect lagging sales that year. Or perhaps not, it's hard to say.

We could keep doing this forever. For those who might think I'm cherry picking, let me be the first to say *every one of these books or series* comes to mind when I think of the last hundred years of classic speculative fiction. Pratchett comes to mind. Pern comes to mind. Speaker for the Dead is almost objectively a better book than its prequel, Ender's Game. The only bias here is that I picked corresponding years. So the moment I found a book published roughly in the same year as the award winner, I stopped.

If this tells you anything, it's simply that the people who care about these genre distinctions care a bit too much in the same way that music critics will come up with some weird genre name in order to be the person who coined it. Fair. But there are dangers with being the person who coins, for instance, the term "manic pixie dream girl" and later apologize on Salon.com for it. If for nothing else because, as I once defended, manic pixie dream girls actually exist out in the wild and are generally really decent people.

In other words, these conversations seem a bit masturbatory in nature. They don't reflect sales, they don't reflect the hearts of readers, they don't even reflect the versatility of authors, who often float around between genres. Though McCarthy desperately refused to identify as "science fiction," though he was writing fiction based directly on climate science, though Hemingway wanted and failed to publish spec fic, I think all of them land where Stephen King lands when he said that he didn't care what they called it — what genre they label him as — as long as they didn't take it away.

And his work has been shelved in *wildly* different parts of the library and bookstore.

To be fair, what these conversations *may* reflect, however, is a kind of maven bias.

That is to say experts or connoisseurs of specific genres (literary, dystopia, cyberpunk, M/M romance) read either only or mostly that genre and then paint whatever they notice in their expertise across the entire industry and culture. But culture isn't a monolith. Nor is it a war. Nor is it even a set of puzzle pieces.

Culture is a biodiverse farm in a biodiverse forest with biodiverse prairie as the slightest border between: all manner of flora and fauna percolate its borders and, now and again, one of those flora or fauna becomes over cultivated enough to become the dominant force. But that doesn't necessarily tell us all that much about the farm in the forest. Especially when cross pollination gets involved.

It just tells us that cultivation is still happening, whether mainstream or subcultures or anything between.

For instance, recently I binge read the *Sun Eater* series with reckless abandon. I was grossly irresponsible. I stayed up until midnight or three in the morning almost every night I read every book. I haven't don't that but for once in college and once in high school. *I do not do this.* And because of my SFWA status, the majority of my friends — who are readers, not writers, and who read very broadly — took me serious when I said that it's the best science fiction series I can imagine recommending outside my top five. That it even beat my top five.

That's why I'm a maven in that space. I'm not

the best maven, but folks who *don't* read that kind of thing all the time *look* to me to recommend something that they can try. They trust me to filter the dross for them as they do for me. (I don't read tons of romance, but on a maven's advice, I picked up *The Notebook* in high school).

To create a kind of bore tide out of that momentum and force the river to run upstream — to think, therefore, that there is some correlating surge of science fiction in the culture — is a kind of cultural projection. That may or may not be true, but the *last* person you want inspecting that kind of thing is the maven.

Guess what?

I stayed up irresponsibly late reading Dostoevsky the year dad died too. And The Road, as I said above.

So when it's a literary maven, that goes double, since many seem blind to the genre conventions within whatever "literary" is and does as well as blind to the "literary" books within the houses of various genres, published by places like DAW and TOR or, that *far* worse blind spot that will be picked up by our great-grandchildren (if the world persists), Indies. It will take so, so much time to filter through the voices of our era and that's one of the great glories of living in a world in which no one necessarily has to go out of print.

I say far worse blind spot because some of the best literary voices in history — Jane Austen, Emily Dickenson, Nathaniel Hawthorne, Proust, Whitman, Sterne, Pound, Woolf, E.E. Cummings, Benjamin Franklin — were self published or indies. Franklin, in fact, unveils a kind of publishing printing bias where works are not considered self-published for him and his nepotistic connections simply because he owned a press. A decent piece could be written asking the question whether money and favors, more than anything, determine the line between traditional and self-publishing, historically, but this is not that piece.

iii. Average per book, per genre may be impossible to determine with the downfall of Author Earnings (unless an anonymous publishing professional wants to post some hard numbers), but we may have some ideas...

I have an ongoing frustration that this data was paywalled off from the general populace, especially when you consider their manifestos early on. But even with that iron curtain, we didn't have the full picture. It certainly proved that Nielsen Bookscan didn't know the whole picture any more than the 6 people responsible for the Nielsen ratings of Conan O'brien's late show reflected the reality of all two million viewers.

Take one example:

I have a buddy who did print on demand long enough that he started bulk ordering beautiful hardbacks from China. Then he bought *his own print on demand printer* and now ships those straight to the distributor. No middle man whatsoever, POD or traditional. He makes thousands of dollars for every author visit just for showing up and reading to kids and then handsells thousands every year. He's not on Nielsen's bookscan with anything close to his actual numbers. Why would he be? What would possibly motivate him to reveal his real sales to anyone? His model just makes it easier for his folks to get his books. I understand: I want the person who wants my book to get it as soon as possible and for my margin (read: royalty) to be as high as possible. If I can sell one book and make $10 or ten books each for 90¢, why wouldn't I favor the one? Why worry about who has access to my *real* numbers unless I'm desperate for an agent? I love hand selling books because I love meeting readers and book clubs and with wildcards like my buddy, there's no telling what his real numbers are. And therefore the real numbers of the industry.

It's far, far more opaque than folks want you to believe.

Don't believe me?

There was a dude at our last Third Saturday Salon (a monthly open for makers house Tara and I have hosted in NYC since 2016) who printed out five copies of his book on his printer and hand stitched hardbacks that afternoon in front of us. Because he can.

That's the world we live in now. He had a new library in an afternoon.

All of that said, and mindful that Author Earnings had more data than Bookscan, even in 2017 — the year of the theatrical releases of *Logan, Guardians of the Galaxy, Wonder Woman, Thor* — author earnings showed this:

TOTAL UNITS in literary works beat the genres. In fact, it beat them when you combine teen, mystery, scifi together. Now that may be a bit deceptive because I think the literary genre in this case may contain some of the others (and I gave more disclaimers than is sane on that front above). But that share of revenue is mind boggling.

And it's the same with audio:

One of the HUGE things their 2016 report showed was this:

That's by publisher type, showing that the majority of literary works were released by Big Five, Amazon, or indie publishers.

But does that paint the whole picture?

Not at all.

Not in the slightest.

I know for instance that *Bell Hammers* would be classically defined as "literary," but to get exposure, it's categorized in several different sections including humor and WWII romance in order to get a hearing.

Do I care what people call it?

No.

I took the Stephen King approach and sold thousands of copies of that one as an indie. Soon to be tens of thousands. That is the case for romance novels that take the Wharton approach, Scifi novels that take the McCarthy approach, thriller novels that take the McMurtry approach and vice versa.

If there was a way to have access to the data, we might get a fuller picture of how many indies are writing what we would consider literary fiction, but trying to sell them on genre shelves. Because I can tell you right now, being a part of the NYC literary scene, there are gobs and gobs of indies writing literary fiction and they sure as hell aren't being represented by that genre breakdown in that chart.

And this, right here, is why I wish I had access to that scraper data.

But my buddy buying his own printer is the canary in the coal mine.

Whatever you think you know about the publishing industry, guess again. There's a wild world out there from pirate presses to scrappy indie one-cut-vinyl audiobooks that you haven't even begun to experience.

2. Related to this, do literary works have a fandom?

There's a great piece by Naomi Kanakia called Highbrow literature has acquired a fandom. To succeed, writers need to manage it.

It's a great piece, but I want to say: *they always have had a fandom*.

The main reason James Joyce and Tolkien scholars get along so well at conferences is both writers's precious care for language and prose and weird etymologies.

This is why Dorothy Sayers — the mystery writer — talked about this in the "power" of the authorial voice, person, work. Eventually, when you release a work into the wild, it starts to manifest in the minds of other makers.

> They can keep their heaven. When I die, I'd sooner go to middle Earth.

— George RR Martin[7]

Imagination *per se* and loci *per se* are the focus of the novelist, not the "real world," which is the purview of the lower sciences and journalism — though the ends of *these ends*, as Bonaventure points out, are also theology.[8] That seems to be Martin's point, though, comparing Heaven to Middle Earth — especially when you consider that Middle Earth, having been written by a Catholic, is more of the biblical ideal than Martin's own earthly concept of heaven and therefore more like heaven, more like *New Creation* precisely because it is sub-creation — particularly the eschatological and antediluvian parts of that story. By some conceptions of the New Heavens and the New Earth, including Tolkien's, *we do go to Middle Earth when we die.* Or something better: the shared loci of the mind of The Author of Life. As the reader meets us in our created work, whether we be as gracious as Tolkien or as psychopathic as Kvothe, so yet we meet no mere human or demiurge, but rather God — the infinite Unity, an ocean of Being, Consciousness, and Bliss — within his.

In other words, if Tolkien's right in his belief, then George gets what he wants when he dies.

We find shared loci most prevalent in fandoms, of course, but not only fan fiction. And in fact, formal causes lead to real objects: fans can purchase the folded steel version of Aragon's sword, the stitched version of Spiderman's suit, or any other ephemera.[9] As Lisa Tuttle (fellow fiction author and former lover of George R.R. Martin) said:

> Writing has been described as a lonely business. Most writers actually like it that way, thank you very much, but still there is that restless urge to share which leads to collaborations, shared worlds, theme anthologies, and round-robin stories. If fantasy and science fiction writers are more prone to this than writers in other fields, maybe that's because we've long had the habit of meeting up for conventions, conferences and writers' workshops. I think of Mary and Percy Shelley, Lord Byron, Clare Claremont and Dr. Polidori gathered together in an Italian villa in the summer of 1816, challenging each other to write horror stories. Mary Shelley's Frankenstein was the most memorable result; yet I can't help wondering what a Byron-Shelley collaboration might have been. Then I remember a roach-infested apartment in Austin in the summer of 1973, where Bill Wallace, Joe Pumilia and I wrote a horror story together. We thought it was brilliant, but didn't manage to find an editor to share our view.[10]

Martin himself had a similar experience writing for fan zines as an early start to his career, first with dittoed copies for superhero zines and then more elaborate worlds involving horror and fantasy.[11] Harlan Ellison did that in his teens, hitchhiking to NYC to give contributor's copies to Lester Del Rey and the rest of the Hydra club. Nerding out never leaves. Anyone who has been to a science fiction convention knows how drastically different it is from a press scrum at a political event. Perhaps *precisely* diametrically opposed, seraphic and diabolic respectively. This is likely because fantasy and science fiction authors deal in universals — in formal causes — that predicate entire genres and subgenres. I'm using "universals" in the classic sense, though I won't here bother to parse Plato's or Aristotle's or anyone else's side of the argument for now. (Not that I'm the expert who could do it anyhow).

All I mean to show is that as we mean *greenness* for the color or *treeness* as the universal for all trees (both in Chesterton's *tree is a tree at last* and Tolkien's *trees are trees*), so too we mean *vampireness* for all vampire stories, *consciousness* for stories about A.I., or *swordness* for sword and sorcery. Not to mention *deals with the devil* for any sort of Faustian bargain, *belly of the beast* for any deep dark hole a protagonist gets into, or even — as Thomas C. Foster says — "if she comes up, it's a baptism."[12] The list goes on, but any of these discussions at both comicon and more professional conferences like The World Fantasy Convention or WorldCon (including their academic papers) sound much more in line with the sorts of discussions going on behind closed doors in any philosophy or theology department. Indeed, these conversations often *are* identical at places like Mythcon — often cross-pollinating: both deal in hypotheticals. The hypotheses of fantasy authors tend to be something like the school of practical philosophy, practical in the Franciscan sense: prompt action over any doubt or delay. I myself gave a talk at one of these conferences arguing that magic reveals the metaphysics of the author.[13] All of these talks at all of these fantasy conferences on the subject of universals led, ultimately, to the assumption of the word "universe" in this context by Don Markstein in 1970 as he more-or-less systematized a way of parsing the idea of a shared universe. By "universe" they mean what I have meant by "shared loci."[14] Internet denizens further systematized this thinking into **Markstein's Criteria**:[15]

1. If characters A and B have met, then they are in the same universe; if characters B and C have met, then, transitively, A and C are in the same universe.
2. Characters cannot be connected by real people — otherwise, it could be argued that Superman and the Fantastic Four were in the same universe, as Superman met John F. Kennedy, Kennedy met Neil Armstrong, and Armstrong met the Fantastic Four.
3. Characters cannot be connected by characters "that do not originate with the publisher" — otherwise it could be argued that Superman and the Fantastic Four were in the same universe, as both met Hercules.
4. Specific fictionalized versions of real people — for instance, the version of Jerry Lewis from DC Comics' The Adventures of Jerry Lewis, who was

> distinct from the real Jerry Lewis in that he had a housekeeper with magical powers — can be used as connections; this also applies to specific versions of public-domain fictional characters, such as Marvel Comics's version of Thor (a Norse god) or DC Comics' version of Robin Hood (a Welsh legend).
> 5. Characters are only considered to have met if they appeared together on-panel in a story.

In these universes, as Lisa Tuttle hinted, not merely fans but authors collaborate to create stories with shared characters, props, places, and all the trappings of a shared loci. When the reader encounters *these* stories, they end up encountering not only the author, but the authority of the collaboration. Something like the fandom.

In certain cases, these can span most of or even the entirety of a given conference operating — properly — as a shared text in microcosm. *Known Space*, *Merovingen Nights* come to mind for fiction examples or perhaps the endless riffs on Cthulu or Sherlock Holmes. Are there not Harry Potter conferences full of critics and fan fictioneers and cosplayers? And did not *Beneath Ceaseless Skies* throw a ten year anniversary party at Baltimore's World Fantasy Convention for everyone who had ever edited, written, read for, or given money to the zine?16 Clearly both Marvel and DC have heavily delineated universes that — due to the deaths of all of the original creators — is nothing more than highly specialized, highly marketed fan fiction.

Once sold along with Star Wars to Disney, the transition into the great compost heap (I mean that positively — as in biodiversity — not negatively as in garbage) of mythologized pantheon is complete. The original creators of Marvel *no longer even live* (Stan Lee and Jack Kirby come to mind) and therefore the blending of fiction and fanfiction that existed so beautifully in the middle ages has, more or less, returned:

> I am inclined to think that most of those who read 'historical' works about Troy, Alexander, Arthur, or Charlemagne, believed their matter to be in the main true. But I feel much more certain that they did not believe it to be false. I feel surest of all that the question of belief or disbelief was seldom uppermost in their minds. That, if it was anyone's business, it was not theirs. Their business was to learn the story. If its veracity were questioned they would feel that the burden of disproof lay wholly with the critic.
>
> Till that moment arrived (and it did not arrive often) the story had, by long prescription, a status in the common imagination indistinguishable — at any rate, not distinguished — from that of fact. Everyone 'knew' — as we all 'know' how the ostrich hides her head in the sand — that the past contained Nine Worthies: three Pagans (Hector, Alexander, and Julius Caesar); three Jews (Joshua, David, and Judas Mac-

cabaeus); and three Christians (Arthur, Charlemagne, and Godfrey of Bouillon). Everyone 'knew' we were descended from the Trojans — as we all 'know' how Alfred burned the cakes and Nelson put the telescope to his blind eye. As the spaces above us were filled with daemons, angels, influences, and intelligences, so the centuries behind us were filled with shining and ordered figures, with the deeds of Hector and Roland, with the splendours of Charlemagne, Arthur, Priam, and Solomon.[17]

And it is the same now with Marvel and DC, more or less: how *well* can you do Captain America? Or Black Panther?

Does not Chabon have a shared universe?

And what about other prize winners?

Christopher Nolan gave his take on Batman and it forced others like Shane Carruth to try and "find his Batman."[18] Though cutting one's teeth in these publishing houses and studios is more a function of money rather than honor, it certainly gets us closer to the idea of riffing on worthies, what Kevin Feige of Marvel calls the "sandbox."[19]

The early — aptly named — *Universal Monsters* allowed Frankenstein, Dracula, The Invisible Man, and Wolf Man to interact. And that universe — that they shared the sandbox — gave King fodder for an entire PhD thesis in *Danse Macabre*, arguing that the four original monster predicate all other horrors, including the literary ones.[20]

Perhaps the most well-known shared loci in the

film world would be the *Star Wars* franchise. *Forgotten Realms* of the Dungeons and Dragons mythos is, perhaps, the most prolifically *used* locus when it comes to collaborative storytelling, in its case more of an improvisational-comedy-meets-back-of-the-napkin-math format involving character sheets and dice. But certainly, role playing games *do not work* unless everyone agrees upon the shared reality, the *Yes, And* of longform improv comedy. Specifically with "Yes, and..." you're not actually *forbidden* from the word "no" in later acts of longform improv, nor is conflict forbidden. Rather you must agree that we are all playing the game of, for instance, a door-to-door toilet salesman. Anyone who doesn't play that game of door-to-door toilet salesman isn't building the improv universe that creates the context that tees up what's funny for the audience.21 In a similar vein, spin-offs have become standard fare for making more money off of successful television shows. And the proto shared loci for animation is, of course, The Mouse. You know the one.22

Perhaps the most fascinating — to me, at least — is the magazine 1632, an alt-history book series that started with Eric Flint and Baen Books. In 1632, the fictional town of Grantville, West Virginia and its power plant are transported in space-time by some alien civilization to central Holy Roman Empire, 1632. The series started with Flint's stand-alone by that title and virtually everything since has emerged through collaborators, whether through website submissions or multiple authors contributing to a "main work."23 But it also includes the *Grantville Gazette*, an anthology — or magazine

— that allows short story contributions from those who submit to the "established canon." Outside of extreme recherché in some obscure academic journal, it's quite possibly the largest quantity of pages a contributor is required to read prior to submitting to any given market.

All of that in mind, what — pray tell — do you call all of these recent Pulitzer Prize winners that retell all our old stories other than fan fiction? Other than a shared universe?

Other than a communal loci? A shared memory artifact that we all discuss?

An embalmed master spirit?

Oh yes, the fandom has always been alive and well in the literary crowd.

Ultimately, these arguments about canon pervade every shared universe and — like any philosophical or theological dialog or really any art or science — make up the borders of what is and isn't allowable within the loci, that shared mind space. They create a trysting place of thought within the Trysting Place of Thought and require prior knowledge (perhaps, in the worst cases, of a Gnostic variety as in the case of Scientology; perhaps, in the best cases, of a Trinitarian variety as in the case of the once-bedridden Christopher Tolkien carrying on his father's standard once his father had fallen beyond the veil) to further the story. Some universes end up stricter than others, but they more or less achieve the same function: *we* mean *this* when we use *these* terms. It's about sharing imagined memories.

George R. R. Martin has an interesting take on this in *A Dance with Dragons*:

> Down here, sleeping and waking had a way of melting into one another. **Dreams became lessons, lessons became dreams**, things happened all at once or not at all. Had he done that or only dreamed it?
>
> "Only one man in a thousand is born a skinchanger," Lord Brynden said one day, after Bran had learn to fly, "and only one skinchanger in a thousand can be a greenseer... once inside the wood they linger long indeed. A thousand eyes, a hundred skins, wisdom deep as the roots of ancient trees. *Greenseers.*"
>
> Bran did not understand so he asked the Reeds. "Do you like to read books, Bran?" Jojen asked him.
>
> "Some books. I like the fighting stories. My sister Sansa likes the kissing stories, but those are stupid."
>
> "A reader lives a thousand lives before he dies," said Jojen. "The man who never reads lives only one. The singers of the forest had no books. No ink, no parchment, no written language. Instead they had the trees, and the weirwoods above all. When they died, they went into the wood, into leaf and limb and root, and the trees remembered. All their songs and spells, their histories and prayers, everything

they knew about this world. Maesters will tell you that the weirwoods are sacred to the old gods. The singers believe they *are* the old gods. When singers die they become bard of that godhood."

"...For men, time is a river," Lord Brynden said, "We are trapped in its flow, hurtling from past to present, always in the same direction. The lives of trees are different... Once you have mastered your gifts, you may look where you will and see what the trees have seen, be it yesterday or last year or a thousand ages past."[24]

As with weirwoods, so with books: we share our memories unbounded from time and live a thousand lives. How appropriate that one's on pulp and the other's in the wood that predicates pulp. That the rings of the trees can be looked at all at once, when hewn, just as any part of the book can be seen flipping pages, any part of the library from selecting any book.

And when you meet the mind of the weirwood, you meet the mind of the greenseer within. Can you change his mind? Carruthers shows the same phenomenon at work in Shereshevski's mind, how he stored his own synesthetically:

> S.'s process of recollection was a process of perception; he mentally walked through his memory places and looked at what was there. This accounts for the

essentially perceptual nature of ancient advice on the preparation of *loci*....

S. was completely uneducated in mnemonics. The system of backgrounds and images he devised was self-taught, refined by trial and error. He never seems to have discovered the principle of "memory for things" that every ancient writer on the subject is at pains to emphasize as the key to the successful composition and delivery of an oration. This, surely, was because his prodigious feats of memory were treated as freakish, and he himself as a vaudeville act, his art perceived to be a mere curiosity without social usefulness and ethical value. **Moreover, he was rewarded only for his iterative accuracy — creative composition was not his aim.**[25]

But it *could* have been composition. And that composition *could* have been shared and subsequently "walked through" by another. As it already had been in the Middle Ages:

> It is clear, both from descriptions of pedagogy and from the practices of individual writers, that much of the process of literary composition was expected to occur mentally, in mature authors, according to a well-defined method that had postures, settings, equipment, and products all its own. The drafts that re-

sulted were designated by different names, which do vary a bit according to the particular writer, but each of which denotes a fairly well defined stage of composition. These are, first, *invention*, taught as a wholly mental process of searching one's inventory. It involves recollection, primarily, and occurs with postures and in settings that are also signals of *meditation*; indeed, it is best to think of invention as a meditational activity, and indeed Quintilian so designates it. This meditation involves both the discovery and the *disposition* of the subject matters, and it results in a product called the *res*, a term familiar also from the pedagogy of memory training. More complete than what modern students think of as their outline, the *res* should, according to Quintilian, be formed fully enough to require no more than finishing touches of ornamentation and rhythm. In other words, the *res* is like the rougher drafts of a composition, with much room left still for shaping, rearranging, and adjustment.26

So the *res*, particularly — for our purposes — in creative works, is rearranging of memories stored in the loci (and, if Synesius, Lewis, and Bonaventure are correct, *the loci itself*) into a rough draft form that becomes an original composition. The *res* is a fully formed rough draft *in the mind*. Focus on that for a moment, because that sort of discipline that any composer made we would associate today with photographic memory. The assumption is that making a *res* could be taught to any writer. Indeed, it was the expected form for all.

> **Medieval reading is conceived to be not a "hermeneutical circle" (which implies mere solipsism) but more like a "hermeneutical dialog" between two memories, that in the text being made very much present as it is familiarized to that of the reader**. Isidore of Seville, we remember, in words echoed notably by John of Salisbury, says that written letters recall through the windows of our eyes the voices of those who are not present to us (and one thinks too of that evocative medieval phrase, *voces paginarum*, "the voices of the pages"). So long as the reader, in meditation (which is best performed in a *murmur* or low voice), reads attentively, that other member of the dialog is in no danger of being lost, the other voice will sound through the written letters. Perhaps it is not inappropriate to recall again, having just spoken of the Petrarch, the Greek verb, ***anagignôskô,* "to read," but literally "to know again" or "remember."**[27]

Reading is to remember again what the author once remembered, to encounter the author's memory *as your own* — as per earlier an author's book *becomes* the reader's experience? That's not merely magic, it's something the most magical and controversial writer of our time — J.K. Rowling — rendered literal in the chapter of *The Goblet of Fire* entitled *The Pensieve*.

Set aside for a moment the fact that Chabon's work has an interconnected universe like all fandom from Vonnegut to King to Sanderson to Marvel.

Any literary work has a fandom. Academic citations are a fandom. Weird little knitting circles on a reading night at the Center for Fiction are a fandom. drDoctor was and is a fandom.

Any time you're remembering the crafted memories of an author *in community*, it's a fandom.

If any of you do anything at all with this piece — talk about it, comment, respond to it, react to it, use it to inspire a story, cut it up and turn it into anti-my-ideas collage — you've made a fandom.

Every MFA program is a fandom.

That's always been the case. Ever shall be, world without end…

a. Do genre books have a stratification of what makes a literature of high achievement?

Absolutely.

Not only do the awards ceremonies show this, but the speculative fiction community is *so obsessed* with adding to the great conversation of their tradition, that if a work comes along and moves it forwards in a significant way, they all rally behind it.

It's wild to watch, but it happens every year. All you have to do is watch the backends of the SFWA board to see it working. The discords. Stuff gets shared with a rocket hot intensity.

And sometimes it's just because it's quirky or fun.

But most often it's because it moves the great conversation forwards.

b. What constitutes a ghetto in genre, in age, in other "sales" categories?

I don't have an answer to this personally, because I don't believe it exists. We've already shown that sales, either way, excludes this. I have no idea why age would contribute to it.

It's quite baffling to me, to talk this way. The Pratchett quote covers this.

c. What is a fandom good for, anyways?

Riffing, thinking, and moving the conversation forwards. Any academic community around a work — Tolkien conferences, Nabokov conferences, Virginia Wolf circles — all do this.

It supports, hopefully, living authors. But it at very least preserves the memories — the embalmed spirits — of the dead ones.

i. What is the nature of the author?

The author is a creature who takes their ideas in the flash of insight — the entire end in the beginning — and who through sub creation and direct presence incarnates their mind through blood sweat and tears into the text so that their ideas will live on in the mind of the reader.

ii. How does a fandom always-already participate in the person and work of the author?

The author has a reader in mind at the start, even if subconsciously. A reader in mind when they're working, someone to share it with. When shared, the reader has in mind not the author as a person, so much, as what the author had in mind.

So it's a weather of the mind that's shared.

The moment one of these readers becomes an author who responds in any way, good or bad, to the author, this is the fandom completing the cycle. A cycle born anew as the original author now becomes the fandom of the reader.

It's a feedback loop with a dual consubstantiality living in shared memory.

d. How might one steward this nature of a fandom?

Read more, write more, but most of all: gather in person and share your contact info.

It's that simple: it's just a matter of groups with a shared rolodex.

3. Are *literary* works — as the term is used in modernism and post-modernity (not, I'll remind you, even in *metamodernism or pre-modernism*) — the norm? Or are genre works the norm?

I think this is unknowable with the current distinction without difference.

4. Your turn.

Tell me what you think, but be civil, please. Here there be dra... children:

Lanceschaubert [at] gmail [dot] com

http://lanceschaubert.org

http://lanceschaubert.substack.com

And subscribe, for the love of all that is good and *literary*.

---

[1]
Quick note: in case you were wondering, this was written as a lecture entitled "Fairy Stories" for the Andrew Lang lectureat the University of St Andrews. It was delivered in 1939, the same year that C.S. Lewis conceived the idea for Narnia (outside of the image of a faun with parcels that he'd had in his head since 1914). I believe, based on that timeline, that this part of the passage inspired Narnia: that Lewis couldn't get the lamppost next to the faun with the packages out of his head. It's possible, of course, that Tolkien was throwing shade on his friend — such critique certainly wasn't be-

neath him and he often and loudly voiced his dislike at the Bird and Baby where the Inkling's met for beer and hash on Tuesday midday, but I doubt it.

2

Kendall Bates, who co-authors this publication, often responds to Marco Rubio's retort "we need more welders and less philosophers" or, as others have said, "we need less philosopher kings and more plumbers," by arguing the counterpoint, "actually we need more philosopher plumbers."

3

To Neo-Passéism's point, above.

4

Seven of them. Kind of like the Chandrian.

5

And Kvothe the Bloodless...

6

Lincoln Michel, "Yes, People Still Buy Books," *Slate*, April 30, 2024, https://slate.com/culture/2024/04/book-sales-publishing-industry-statistics-substack-penguin-lawsuit.html.

7

"On Fantasy | George R.R. Martin," July 11, 2016, originally published in The Faces of Fantasy: Photographs by Pati Perret copyright © 1996 by Pati Perret http://web.archive.org/web/20160711062020/http://www.georgerrmartin.

com/about-george/on-writing-essays/on-fantasy-by-george-r-r-martin.

8

St. Bonaventure, *On the Reduction of the Arts to Theology*, trans. Zachary Hayes, O.F.M., Works of St. Bonaventure (Ashland, Ohio: Bookmasters, 1996).

9

An entire YouTube channel entitled *Make It Real* exists to manifest fantasy objects in our world. Of course, this begs the question: wasn't it real in the first place? Need production costs and capabilities be the only predicates for realness? Disney seems to have ignored this possibility.

10

"Writing Together | George R.R. Martin," June 25, 2016, http://web.archive.org/web/20160625081834/http://www.georgerrmartin.com/about-george/on-writing-essays/writing-together-by-lisa-tuttle/.

11

"Why I'm Here Today, or, Secrets of My Black Past | George R.R. Martin," July 27, 2016, http://web.archive.org/web/20160727191758/http://www.georgerrmartin.com/about-george/speeches/why-im-here-today-or-secrets-of-my-black-past/.

12

Thomas C. Foster, *How to Read Literature Like a Professor: A Lively and Entertaining Guide to Reading Between the Lines* (HarperCollins, 2017).

13

"Speeches, Readings, Debates, and Radio Hours with Lancelot Schaubert • The Showbear Family Circus," The Showbear Family Circus, accessed August 9, 2020, http://lanceschaubert.org/about-lancelot/speaking-readings-conferences-lancelot-schaubert/.

14
THE MERCHANT OF VENICE meets THE SHIEK OF ARABI, by Don Markstein (as "Om Markstein Sklom Stu"), in *CAPA-alpha* #71, September 1970;, accessed August 9, 2020, http://toonopedia.com/universe.htm.

15
"Shared Universe," in *Wikipedia*, July 13, 2020, https://en.wikipedia.org/w/index.php?title=Shared_universe&oldid=967456865.

16
"World Fantasy 2018 Program Guide," accessed October 8, 2021, https://wfc2018.org/konopas/.

17
C.S. Lewis, *The Discarded Image* (Cambridge: Cambridge University Press, 1994).

18
"Buckle Your Brainpan: The Primer Director Is Back With a New Film | WIRED," accessed April 4, 2021, https://www.wired.com/2013/03/primer-shane-carruth/.

19
Adam Rogers, "How Marvel Unified Its Movie Universe (and Why That Won't Be Easy for DC)," *Wired*, accessed April 4, 2021, https://www.wired.com/2013/08/kevin-feige-marvel-dc-movies/.

20
Stephen King, *Danse Macabre* (Simon and Schuster, 2011).

21

Matt Besser, Ian Roberts, and Matt Walsh, *The Upright Citizens Brigade Comedy Improvisation Manual* (Comedy Council of Nicea, LLC, 2013).

[22] "Shared Universe," in *Wikipedia*, July 13, 2020, https://en.wikipedia.org/w/index.php?title=Shared_universe&oldid=967456865.

[23] "1632 Series," in *Wikipedia*, August 1, 2020, https://en.wikipedia.org/w/index.php?title=1632_series&oldid=970565320.

[24] George R. R. Martin, *A Dance with Dragons* (Bantam Books, 2015), 494-503.

[25] Mary Carruthers, *The Book of Memory: A Study of Memory in Medieval Culture* (Cambridge University Press, 2008), 98.

[26] Mary Carruthers, *The Book of Memory: A Study of Memory in Medieval Culture* (Cambridge University Press, 2008), 241.

[27] Mary Carruthers, *The Book of Memory: A Study of Memory in Medieval Culture* (Cambridge University Press, 2008), 243-249

Also by Lancelot

- Substack essays and short fiction
- Of Gods and Globes I
- Of Gods and Globes II
- Of Gods and Globes III
- Overmorrow — *lyrical urban fantasy*
- Bell Hammers: The True Folk Tale of Little Egypt — *historical humor novel*
- Tap & Die — *a "Die Bard" fantasy novella*
- 15 Vale Short Stories — *short stories from the universe where all of his fiction and nonfiction and poetry and photonovels connect*
- The Greenwood Poet — *poetry written during the pandemic in Greenwood cemetery, 500 acres of the oldest rural cemetery in America*
- Inconveniences Rightly Considered — *poems from his twenties*
- Harry Rides the Danger — *children's picture book on courage*
- The Elevator Out — *children's picture book on wonder*
- *H.A.L.T.S.* — *90's alt-rock folk album*
- *All Who Wander* — *indie folk, experimental album*
- *Open* — *short film written for WRKR productions*

- *Cold Brewed — photo novel (graphic novel with still photographs) in a world where the prohibition made third wave coffee illegal*

Over at http://lanceschaubert.org you can find the archive of 400 academics, artists, and authors published in The Showbear Family Circus, resources for your own creative work, as well as ongoing serialized work by Lancelot.

Thanks for buying, reading, and sharing the work of living authors.

www.ingramcontent.com/pod-product-compliance
Lightning Source LLC
Chambersburg PA
CBHW052121070526
44586CB00016B/2029